Life Opens Up Like a Flower

Life Opens Up Like a Flower

by Dede Meltzer

For Sarah and Gal,
Enjoy these poems!
♡ Dede
6-28-2022

RoseDog 🐾 Books
PITTSBURGH, PENNSYLVANIA 15238

RoseDog Books
585 Alpha Drive
Suite 103
Pittsburgh, PA 15238
Visit our website at *www.rosedogbookstore.com*

ISBN: 978-1-63661-572-1
eISBN: 978-1-63661-601-8

Library of Congress Control Number: 2021922660

Cover Art: Photograph, "Garden Tulips" by Anonymous
Back Cover Photo of Author: By Ray Smith

To contact the author or author's agent regarding permissions, readings, presentations, guest lecturing by the author, or other forms of literary engagement, please email lifeopensuplikeaflower@yahoo.com.

Contents

Wash Me in the River

Wash me in the river
of your love—
a language unspoken,
a full universe of movement.
Words are dynamic,
children of the physical.
Words live above,
in the mystical.
How are they collected like   ***s*t*a*r*s***
prosodies of light?
What purpose do they serve?
Are they prisms to refract the night?
Where do we fit in?
How are we connected to them?
What circles do they form?
What declensions are kin?

Are words round as circumferences of a pen or a sun
or are they a gas
we inhale?
Where is the nerve?
Which stresses and syllables people your mindscape
to create new land?
Where is the synapse—
the space in G-d's hands?

I am a poet and I want to change
your language, change your mind,
and persuade your sense
of senses divine.

Rise

Never, ever forget this feeling of connectedness—
fill up every microsecond,
nanos of noneness—
no one to vanish.

The minute you wake up in the morning,
remember this feeling.
Act, act, act—arch your body—
seize this feeling.
Magnify, glorify and regale this feeling—
this sensation, this reeling.
Make this feeling

the center of your life.
This feeling is the story
of the question:
what is your relation
to *Tikkun Olam*—the phrase that denotes
the repairing and the mending of the world—
the fixing for the future,
the alterations made to preserve the "O"
and the "Oh" and the Zero
of negativity converting to one.
Binomials
which we choose—
one or the other, mother or enemy—
and we grow out of the ruse.
Create the tree
from root to bud,
and branches or leaves inbetween.

Push out the force as a woman in labor,
giving birth to the next children.
Memes and immergence
hum into unity of purpose.
Food morsels from the picnic table are passed down the line.
Peace—aah, joy; a cluster of association, verification and revisitation
to intoxicate the head.
Blame what libations
on the slough, the sloughed, and the slaying
that came before to clear the proscenium
for play.

We are playful as puppies.
We are grown to
romp untrammeled
fields, wild swaying flowers
of grasses, the blades' tall yellows dancing
en masse to rhythms of wind and showers.

Clouds storm and lightening
bolts strike the mind
amidst mist in the morning.
Live the dream
as if the mourning for you
were over, the bell sounded
in the reverberations of five a.m.,
before the sunlight gleams—
RISE, RISE, RISE
from your bed.

It Started with a Star

It started with a star.
It is a time of learning,
S c r I bb l e S c r abb le
    and

     dance.
I must take my chances
  Now,
   Now,
    Now—
Forge a theater
 and combine.

I have such a better love now.

I am so deeply happy—
so   deeply,   deeply
    happy.

Every last and first cell and sunshine nucleus
you've touched through your love,
your gaze—the ways you answer me.
You hear me.
How do we inspire
one another?
My lover,
we have a romance
from **angels but** *for* **the world,**
being for this world
more healing and stronger

than the forces of war.

WE HAVE A LOVE TO TRANSCEND
the divorce of mind from heart.
WE HAVE A LOVE TO TRANSCEND
the divorce of Science from Art.

Yes, it started with a star—
a star loved for its brilliance and form from afar—
a star pondered for hours and years
millenia ago—
a star understood better
and known for its faithfulness
and the unexpected revelation
of relation over space and the movements of
time to other celestial bodies
luminescent on the face of night.

Three Birds I Saw

I.

Three birds I saw
through the window pane.
They flew as surprise
to my passing train.

The seagulls came out large
over Newark Bay,
owning sky as undercharge
for pollution that was man-made.

Under the cloudy sky,
the red painted building of a factory sits
on a peninsula of sewage,
quiet smokestacks and grit.

II.

Three words you said
were the magic key
that I hold in my hand
fastidiously.

Those words—"I love you"— loom large as lights.
They let me see
straight up a million flights,
spiralled to heaven: glory.

You rock, you ride, and you splice
the end into beginning,
and roll ivory dice,
settling on knowing and telling

the way time will reveal
the invisible
in leap after leap
after leap—

oh, the miracle of each call—
until trust is born
out of atoms small,
or nothing at all.

III.

Three songs I heard
before I understood
what aims I'd shirked
and how to push good

into the realm of reality:
send her out like a grown child,
clothed and fed—ready
to toss those rules which she reviled,

and to replace the piecemeal corporate view
of the bottom line

with the dictates of oxygen,
food, and knowledge for children;

and with adherence to love:
the one—
truth,
and not Sublime.
As new leaders expand the power of *can*,
feel the weight
of wisdom
on a long hand.

Let us convoke in circle to create peace.
Dissemble the matrix
of politics and greed.
Act in the awe of hope and need.

Why You Slept Twice

How do you explain the fact
that someone is not here?

Why did you sleep twice,
waking up from the second round
as if in the first
you had never slept at all,

as if in the first—too uncomfortable,
the mattress too hard—your muscles were crushed—
your dancer's thighs stultified
and made sore for naught;

as if because when you awoke
you knew,
although you felt fine,
it wasn't a *real* sleep

because it was not your bed;
you slept there out of laze
or the subconscious quest for solace
relying on love and dream as haze.

Yet when you awoke
your rest was disclaimed
in the mist's clearing
by all the voices around you,

and you took it to your head—
and so you slept again.
You awoke the second time having truly rested,
knowing the dreams were yours

and reality was indeed sublime,
and that your understanding—
this new state of being—
could not by a soul be unmoored.

When you awoke,
your joy—your direction this time—
was so self-aware inside and out,
it shone like a rainbow for peace arching

over sky. No, it could not be denied,
with you knowing the import
for the long term, with you knowing
the spring was sprung.

You are, alas, sent beyond
the voices of doubt that did you harm.

How Can I Explode
My Works into Space-Time?

How can I explode my works into space-time?
I've a sense it will happen the way a star,

like the sun, would shed its sphericity,
letting the burning gases loose to streak, orange,

yellow, red, azul blue fire, racing endless masks,
like hooks of solar fingers, dark across dusty

galactic sky. I've a sense that the multi-verses
are a realm of real estate that I managed to buy.

I've a sense it will happen as I stay close
to the graphic forms I trust, envisioning that I signify.

I shall just work through the letters, their sphericities
and segments of lines. Broken as they are, I mend them, to reach a rhyme.

So Wide the Lateral Moves

So wide are the lateral moves
    juxtaposing parochialities,
    disturbing unperturbedness
of mind—from one
coast, across a country,
to the other.

Bona fide, again I feel,
to recall my cousins who reside in L.A.,
'cause one came East
for a visit on the holiday,
and we chatted on the phone
the other day.

I am earning my degree—
a sense of equality to call
upon, to interact, to further
the globe of networks of knowledge—
able agents of hope and movements,
of my beloveds in spirit, in mind, in heart;

of my peers, of my collegial league
of lovers of arts, my posses, my cat's
cradles letting goals lost be
remembered. I have recalled persons and faces
of my green, my verdant river banks and crossings—
I regard the lushness of successes.

Let us abandon the idiocy of a dominion of unreflection,
of a dull iron rule cast over a parent, cast over a spouse,
cast over a younger, cast over the other—

who says we are all meant dumbly
to bite our lips—
in fright,
as fools?

Unrefreshed is the past—
the heavy, rusted chain that linked us.
You know not who you are,
with your bully streak leaching,
seeping in; come nocturnal moments of assault.

I, good-bye, say—and look deeply, so deeply at the faults in your tongue
that lies, geographic in its transference of shame to innocents—
and the faults, the screams
in your hollow house—
and the injuring pavement
of your circular drive.

Make way for my new day. I am the insured,
the guaranteed, and the muscled,
defending myself with a kick and a fall,
and a run fast to the car, accelerating with my own
lithe muscles, into spirit—into trust,
fast into the blithe willingness of art and words.

Poems are Marbles

Poems are marbles,
shot from the hand—
the force of opposing fingers
and friction
send them out
into the grand forum,
the packed dirt of a schoolyard;
or onto the floor of some room,
carpeted like a library
or festooned
as a banquet hall;
or ejected onto a grey cement sidewalk
by children near their house;
or as a homeless family
in a world unannounced.

Poems are marbles.
We send them out.
They knock into one another,
make contact
and start a chain.
Sometimes they even ricochet
off of some unusual edge.
They wait quietly on the ground
till more come
and reconfigure the dust.
They push each other around and bully the air
as much or as little as they can.
They entertain in small arenas

for those who play.
They don't stay the night:
their game is day.

Poems are marbles.
They are not of clay.
They are made of glass, the delicate material,
yet they are hard and impenetrable
by ordinary means—
inscrutable
to some, it seems,
for whom the white swirls are clouds to vision.
Others don't mind the mystery,
remain in awe
of the smooth, round shape,
respecting the scale unmarred.

The marbles form a matrix,
a sort of ring.
They glide in relation to each.
They form a mean—
some complex of patterns—
an intersection of colliding directions and trajectories—
sound, tone, image, figure, voice and theme—
assembling a community of clues.

Eventually they pay dues:
the implicit reason is to stay in the club.
Marbles are exclusive.
They rule their hub—

a haughty institution
with a universal sense
of street and resolution,
of justice and the shaping of future hence.

Montezuma Refuge

Three flocks of birds
are moving fast,
elliptically,
back and forth
across the road,
flying amidst
their nature preserve.

I left my bag on purpose
in the car.
Two keys—
one to the ignition
and one to the doors—
are all that I carry
while I do the necessary thing:
I place myself in the scene.

Observe and absorb:
this is the truth of which
a creator means,
and I am passing this way
because ten minutes before,
I recalled my ex-spouse's
pearled words,
"Never get out of a place
on the same path
you came in."

Undisputing the wisdom,
I ventured up Route 89,

where I had landed, unplanned,
after dropping off a sweet co-
celebrant of my friend,
a bride-to-be,
after the feting for her—
a bridal shower
where we guests sat
in foldable beach chairs
outdoors, near the shoreline
of Seneca Lake.

But here they are—
racing in my midst:
three flocks of birds
moving fast,
elliptically,
back and forth,
like an ongoing conversation.

Here, externalized,
are the continuous ecologies
that my lover provoked,
that my lover stores,
that my lover has smoked—
and that cause me to release
these words onto a page.

He, a traveller, a trainer of animals,
lives in the city
where from his studio he has

explained the acrobatics of a flock
of downstate carrier pigeons
as reflecting the work of a trainer.
Here, upstate, where I am touring,
are lither birds electing themselves
repeatedly with busy wings and song
to traverse inbetween and hence adjoin
the low trees that rise
among brown-headed, quiet reeds.

Waterproof Feathers

Waterproof feathers,
in case you didn't notice,
are the only kind I wear.

In case you didn't notice, they are
the only kind I know; they are
my means of unusual

transport; they are
the legendary stuffs
of ceremonial pillows;

they are the magical parts,
multitudinous,
with which time appears and love sighs,

and with which
I marry
the future.

They are some kind of gambit,
but I don't think you
noticed.

Hearing Sounds: An Ode to Robert

Hearing sounds—
the click rattle of a single cicada
in the city,
the fast drip of a kitchen faucet
into
round plates,
rounded out
by the whish
of a car
passing drums
and lessons
in the lunar rhythm
of lights and nights
to be seized—
through and after the rain.

See the Spike of my Spunk

See the spike of my spunk.
You thought I didn't play
'cause I paid you all the respect
and you never gave it back to me.
My mistake was I didn't insist
on your acknowledging the shifts
and didn't refer you back
to your secret strikes, your hypocritical hits,
your private punches, your tawdry tack—
you are wack.
Oh, I am so glad to be free,
alive with my wits and curiosity.

I shall never fear you,
and I will always fight
your disabuse of me,

for you've played with me
politics as Machiavelli.
You've utilized me, but
who is the means to whose end?
Hell we know philosophy.
My strut down the street is revenge.
I show you how I might take an eye for an eye,
but the brutes I transcend.
Hope and faith I embrace and portend.

I'll call every spade a spade.
I watch it all
and define my world.

I call your violations;
I am fair judge,
honest official, blowing my whistle
and now I am fair to myself:
I don't let you run my life.
I don't let fear break my flight.
As seer or prophet
I reach for vision and make decisions
in the black of the deep, cool night.

9-1-1

Exaltation of patterns of love:

O-

pen

up your mind = turn it around again.

Prick the cells—which of the tests is blood on your

finger shaped into a maroon round

bead?

Wait:

a drop of A plus (+) indicating

the brilliance of student and teacher, the one

who transforms life through interjection,

through infusion for the protection of the whole.

Twin Sonnets

The compleat union
of man and woman
occurred
in the crux of crumbled twin worlds.
It occurred with all the parts,
all the instruments laid out
on the table,
with love as invisible surgeon,
with G-d as creator of meaning
and verve. It happened as a genesis of words—
as the birth of streams
rushing to soothe burns and gashes
and wash away ashes
that many would hold in urns.

It is happening still
as the Big Bang
refurls—
an entire universe in body and head
is and was and is
born
and born again while gravity vanishes
and manifests and
turns
the color of passion and blood—
red.

**Beginning,
beginning,**

beginning again.

Screaming Love

Screaming love I know now.
You voice to me the faults
      which I know are true.
You give me the chance to see myself
        clarify what I must do,
and so I think of you.

Screaming love lives in boxes
where mangled papers never see the light,
where poetry resides in one borough's night.

Screaming love lives in a loft
where the getting
      down to the varnished grit
of the bursting planked floor
precedes the voicing of the quest:
    I want to know who you are.

Screaming love is the perfect stillness
I gave you in suspending the tens
of questions that danced in my head.

Screaming love is the color of rage
at the his-story of injustice,
at the blind chaining of a name.

Screaming love is the way we boarded the bus.
It is the way I turn the page

and the way you turn my mind

                  over and over

                            so many times.

Screaming love is every angle riding in
as we listen to meridians.
It is my hand waving over the heat of your body
as you dream and sleep—you are sanctified.

Screaming love is how I pray for you
with every silent fiber of my being.

The Dance of Words

Poetry is the dance of words
performed like a belly dance
in black accoutrements, tassels and cords
enticing pull as if to draw a shade;
or a ballet danced in red satin slippers:

passion foretold in the word *may*—
or a tango commanding Latin rhythm
with desire's permission.
Poetry is the accent of the cha-cha
and the movement of hips

or the one-two-three waltz of syllables
or the samba's massaging
of feet in contact with floor.
Poetry is the masseuse
of lyric and lore.

It is truth and hope withstanding
the bullfight's gore.
Poetry is the cloth
waved by the matador:
catching the bull's eye.

Poetry is children's games of hide and seek
behind rhododendron—magenta flowering bushes—
and the bark rivulets of an oak tree's trunk,
a tree rooted deeply in the front yard,
against the color grey.

Poetry is the play
of light on walls,
forming shadow in the day.
Poetry is the way
an astute observer

would say my eyes smile,
and my brow is confirmed
when the mind captures new turf
and new bridges are learned,
constructing themselves in the brain.

Poetry is the call to stay
right here, planted on Earth,
and to live life as deep
as the cold, blue Arctic,
remembering past and future in one sweep.

Poetry is the flirting,
the expectation and the knowing.
It is the consummation and the showing.
It is the surprise, the laughter and the rise
of who we were, who we shall be,

and where we, the birds, the lions and the breeze
moving long grasses
all might be going.
Poetry is the possibility
of loving.

Whatchyou gonna do, girl?

Whatchyou gonna do, girl,
all bound up
in unrusted dreams?
Ashes are stoked by irons
in the fire suffered by reams of words—
oh, to climb trees with agility.

Your friends are in their own
contests of dance
to record chance,
and in the process,
the stasis of hands
signals to feet.

Somewhere in the tissue of time
the extremities meet.

Georgia on Metaphor

Lead your life
like Georgia's lecture on metaphor:
come in like a piece of fire from the sky.
Equate mind with acrobat
and define yours, and your
figure as transference
in rhetorical and physical sense.
Wake your audience up into presence
of personhood, politics and ideas.
Make them understand
who you are
as an arrived star.

Strut your evidence
as a cool world-class fighter
or million-dollar attorney would.
Use every relevant bit
you've selected and collected and thought through
by serendipities and intentions
so that you forge the whole.
Imprint it with your stamp,
your authenticity born as the universe went bang.
Insist on the re-enactment
as a first time: as a mind and body storm.
Prove to the watching and listening others
the reality of your form.

The Matrix does not Disappear

When are you going to get it right,
close the gap between your visions and your life?
When are you going to understand
that the matrix of real goodness will not disappear?

It's like the silver quarter
Grandper would pull from behind your ear:
it's always somewhere in the hand
or up the sleeve.

It's never too far
from the temporary tears
that stream down your face,
and it reveals itself anew.

I am an Abrahamist, and I love what that means.
It means I strive for perfection of my deeds.
It means I cling to life's great leafy tree—
and I don't abandon it at half-past three
simply to get some tea—
or, if I do, to take a rest,
then I come right back at my best.

Stay the child, climbing on limbs,
or become the child if you never did it.
Be a swinger of birch branches as was my poet-model
of New England, Mr. Robert Frost, whose verses
talk and walk deep into woods.

I keep my intentions in mind and configure
new forms of a poet's pride—that of
a woman's guarding and serving
the sacred flame, the eternal light.

How Can I Begin?

How can I begin
to tell you what I see
when you gaze at me
with the force of an ocean,
washing over my body like a tidal wave?
You, Atlantic man, are pacific in nature,
and you are Atlantis, the fabled lost land, too;
and you are a thousand stars
up and burning so bright and hot,
a billion years of light in the sky;
and you here are the dendrites in the grey
matter we call *brain*,
connecting cells, people and the air
with your electricity;
you are one who is making a home out of a city
       under siege—
changing skylines of the mind,
opening doors and windows,
      smashing simultaneously.

I love you, great man of power, intellect and feeling.
You, expressive, extremely impressive—
you, immortalizing your vision,
possess and enact your mission.
You are my decision, the beginning of fruition,
a vast whole plain of wild horses;
you are the main.
You are the nexus of many rivers,
born and borne of pain.
I am your refrain.
Come to me again and again.

What Unfolds

What unfolds is answer upon answer
to question upon question upon quest.
What expands is the space of possibilities
 surrounding a synapse.
What grows are the neurons
 connecting split halves of the brain.
What builds is the bridge
 cleaving to rain
till the mind and the cranium are tickled into base,
in a euphoric integration of desire and pace,
to bring two worlds or three into the intersecting
eye, aye, I—open the third one, this chakra of spirit.

Focus carries reason and transports rhyme
in the course of currents in the world here divine.
In the pulse of your love I live and die
a thousand seconds, a thousand isles, a thousand times.
You cast a thousand smiles—you throw a thousand pounds of weight.
Wait to keep it home; keep it real
for you and me—
a thousand tears of joy anticipate the night.

The patience of knowledge ebbs slowly
and regularly as tide over dream,
ocean spreading over ridges of sand.
                  Fill me up—
the air and the mist provide
a thousand reasons why
my outer circle just encountered cry,
to sing the promise,

the hope,
the pearl,
the goal
of you: my Tiger wild.

The white waiting fibers colored in bright
       Mango, Papaya and Lime—
       juice and pastel—
our worlds converge.
Heaven and Earth merge
in water pushing
out hatred into dissolution,
washing away war with
undulating waves.

I am a thousand nymphs and you are Poseidon blue,
with reeds and vines connecting the underworld subconscious
oysters in shells with hidden treasures—
sand dollar anemones and dawn-tinted coral
come up to the surface of the sea—
to seagulls overhead,
to tree trunks travelling high,
to treetops,
       green carpets to welcome
touch, to invite sky;

and shower like lips upon lips—
mine upon yours and yours upon mine,
in the paradise of mind,

like body melding body
in the union of woman and man,
tasting the skin of contrasts intertwined,
rough-smooth, dimpled-silken.

I watch the weather now
as it caresses my garden of flowers
with sunlight, humidity and rain.

The Last Day of Chains

Today was the last day of chains.
The last link was cut
with a long metal implement—
a scissor of two bars edged with blades.
The spades are escaping in the nocturnal haze.
The moon is a mysterious yellow that, like me,
people and animals have seen
for hundreds of thousands
                    upon thousands of years.
Fish and octopi, I wager,
could and can see glimmers of lunar light
flashing and beaming down into the sea somehow—
or do and did the reflections only bounce
for thee?

Who were they
that kept my secret—charisma—for those hidden years—
and I made myself hostage
to their image of me?
Oh, the rebellion is constant—
it shall permeate my hair.
It shall gain weight in the presence of air.
Yes, I shall at last make my own lair,
manage my throne:
if I am a princess, then from whence is
royalty shone?

Yes, the secret is the power of my body,
a gift of long denied.

How can I reach out
and obliterate the sidewalk via serpentine delights;
engage in acrobatics for the expanding brain?
Why must we walk in uncurved lines,
when the truest state is sheer ellipse?
Circle, beta and grace,
I lift and kneel, cross and cross
over white cement—
reverse, reverse, turn and dent.
Do we behave like cars up for rent,
available to be driven, but only in convention's sense?
Are we driven only on highways that incise earth's transcendence?
Oh, dance, dance, dance:
we've got to escape.

We've got to run before and under
the wild setting of the sun,
before we break Nature—shatter her like glass,
before she turns off like an artificial light
for all her strength and bounty.
Nature is subject to the universal delicacy:
she has limits; she has needs.

If we of all faiths or of no faith look under the hoods
of oligarchs, queens, kings, presidents, prime ministers and senates,
we can see what is bad and what is good.
Yes, we can use our physical, intellectual and moral stamina
to quit our addiction to economies of meat, plastics and fossil fuels.

A true representative republic would favor
the wind and the sun as sources of power.
This is our hour to repair earth's abused condition
and allow sensibility to overtake irresponsible leaders'
reckless decisions.
Yes, it's remake, remake, remake and revision.
Belie the known consequences of unchange.
Call out false beauty by name.
Show your vision.
The choices we have now, at this moment of reckoning,
will disappear if we don't embrace Truth,
and reduce America's, China's and India's greenhouse gas emissions.

We, the people who inhabit Earth today, can avert apocalypse
if we trim our systems' carbon-dioxide and methane gas emissions—
lowering our methane and carbon footprint on the planet,
and sparing the rainforests, too.
This twenty-first century decade of the twenties
is when companies and governments shall invest
our money into ways to capture CO-2 directly from the air.

That is this free citizen's proposition for universal freedom.
Besides our lifestyle changes—
what we choose to purchase and to eat, what we choose to wear
and what we choose to construct and repair—
we need effective government agencies, corporations and institutions
with labs for inventions to accomplish our freedom and avert doom.

I am Reborn in the Morning

I awoke at two o'clock
a.m.,
circles of energy stacked upon
my chest,
arguing overwhelmingly
yesss, yesss, yessssssss.
Pull me up
out of bed—I rise,
levitated. I feel like Jesus
resurrected from his cross,
arms, limbs, floating to lead
me into what compels
    my new life.
I am no longer wife
to the notion of incompetence
and vanished confidence.
I am reborn in the morning
in the aftermath of desire

              y
            r
           o
           t
           c
            e
           j
            a
          r
           t
    long
  a
on

an eternal flame glows
in the wake of our tryst.
　　I feel not alone.
I feel, I comprehend, meridians of power,
connecting me every minute, second and hour
to the rest of Creation. Humanity is balanced by
showers of rain, streams of sunlight,
jungle gorillas,
burnt-orange and black tigers,
lions of the yellow plains,
elephants on the run.
I hear the whales courting
one another in a watery kind of love.
I am one with the atlas,
the greatest depth of ocean seeming to exceed
in length the highest peak of mountains
that we see. There is more unseen than seen
in the body of me.

Two hours later,
I go to sleep again.
I awake at eight.
A sleight of magic
possesses my hands
to sense skin turned silken
under your influence.

It is no longer my body.
It is Beauty.
It is yours,
bathing in the sensation of touch.

Life Opens Up Like A Flower

Life opens up like a flower.
We push, we push, we push
and do not cower
to show the beauty,
attract the bee,
expose ourselves to wind;
feel the accumulation of time's power—
let the attraction begin.

Jumping in relation and association,
pollen swirling infinities
pull out experience,
converting loss to win,
meshing knowledge into life,
diving into and divining
the secret, perfumed air
where stamen and pistil
are sworn to fate,
where many means are excluded
in the fashioning of bait,
where long evolution is worn
in petal and leaf born
of ancient lightning storms,
beckoning only the right
insect-thieves
where that way unique
shall bring the world beyond war—
into peace,
and shall bring the globe

from the woo of season
and the tangle of warm air
into Nature's full repair.